The Art of Dining Well

Everything You Need to Know to Shine at the Table

The Art of Dining Well

Everything You Need to Know to Shine at the Table

Patricia Napier-Fitzpatrick

Copyright @ 2020 by Patricia Napier-Fitzpatrick

All rights reserved. No part of this book may be reproduced in any manner whatsoever without written permission except in case of brief quotations embodies in critical articles of reviews. For more information, address The Etiquette School of New York at 243 Elm Street, Southampton, NY 11968.

Visit our Website at www.etiquette-ny.com

ISBN 978-0-578-62480-8

FIRST EDITION: JANUARY 2020

In Memory of my parents,

Maxine and William K. Napier,

with love and gratitude

The art of dining well is no slight art; the pleasure, not a slight pleasure.
- Michel De Montaigne, *Essays*, 1588

Contents

Preface · xi
Introduction · xiii

1 Table Settings and How to Read Them · 1
2 Taking a Seat, Conversation, and Posture at the Table · · · · · · · · · 5
3 The Napkin: The Silent Signal · 11
4 Styles of Eating—American and Continental · · · · · · · · · · · · · · · 15
5 Forms of Service: Dinner is Served! · 27
6 The Courses and How to Eat Them · 31
7 The Asian Style of Eating—Eating with Chopsticks · · · · · · · · · · 49
8 Stemware, Beverages, and Toasts · 55
9 Patricia's Rules for the Table · 63
10 How to Eat Certain Foods · 67
11 Entertaining at Home: Courteous Host and Gracious Guest · · · · 75
12 Entertaining for Business: Host and Guest Protocol · · · · · · · · · · 79
13 The Restaurant Staff: At Your Service · 85
14 Gratuity Guidelines · 89

Preface

Among my most cherished memories of childhood are the hours spent at meals with my five brothers and sisters and my mother and father. The kitchen was the center of our universe growing up—from the first thing in the morning when we would gather around the table for breakfast to the end of the day when we eagerly awaited the arrival of our father to come home from the office to have dinner at 6:00 p.m.

It was in the kitchen that we not only learned the rules of table manners and how to hold our silverware but where we also learned to converse. We would talk about our day, local happenings, and generally learn something new and interesting from my entertaining, well-read, intellectual father.

For holidays, special occasions, and dinner with friends and relatives, we would eat in the formal dining room. It was always a rather anxious time for us—the children—because we knew that we had to be on our very best behavior and not embarrass our mother who had tried so hard to instill in us the importance of proper decorum at the table.

Although all my siblings live in different cities in the United States now, we still enjoy a wonderful camaraderie when we meet for reunions every year or so. When we gather around the table for meals and lively conversation, it's as if time has stood still.

Meals with my daughter and husband followed a different pattern in these more-modern, hectic times. The three of us were seldom able to have breakfast or lunch together every day, but we always tried to have dinner together.

I know this seemingly simple act of sharing meals together is just as important now—if not more so—for making families feel close and keeping each other abreast of what is going on in their lives. I hope that my daughter will look back on her childhood and the many meals we shared together with as much fondness as I do of mine.

Since I founded The Etiquette School of New York, I have conducted countless dining etiquette classes for individuals of all ages and nationalities—from young children to corporate executives. It has been a wonderful experience for me to meet and help so many people. It is particularly gratifying to me when I receive thank-you notes from clients telling me that my lessons have improved their confidence in themselves, and their enjoyment of dining with their friends, family, and colleagues.

I thoroughly enjoy teaching the fundamentals of dining etiquette and hope that with this book, I can impart this valuable knowledge to all who might seek it, and with whom I cannot meet in person.

Introduction

The meal is the emblem of civilization. The most important human relationships are all celebrated with or nourished by the sharing of food. What would one know of life as it should be lived or nights as they should be spent apart from meals?
-James and Kay Salter, Life is Meals

Since prehistoric times, human beings have gathered around one kind of table or another to share their meals with family, friends, and colleagues. From the very first society—the "Hunting and Gathering Society"—the communal "sharing" of food has been a ritual practiced by civilized societies. Of course, the way the food has been eaten, where it has been eaten, as well as the type of food and its preparation, has become more highly stylized with each passing generation.

Although not all historians agree, some trace the origins of classic fine dining to the aristocratic family of the sixteenth century, the Medici's of Florence. When Catherine de Medici married Henry I in 1533, her dowry included several dozen dinner forks wrought by Benvenuto Cellini, the great Italian silversmith.

The modern-day table setting is attributed to Charles I of England, who is 1633 declared, "It is decent to use a fork," a statement that heralded the beginning of civilized table manners. But the French court of Louis XIV truly elevated dining to an art form.

The eating habits and food culture of each nation vary with respect to their civilization, customs, and cultures. Food and eating represent the culture of countries. Most countries outside of the United States, spend a lot more time at meals—sometimes hours; and they savor the conversation and company as much as they do their food and wine—particularly in Italy and France.

As Charles Sanderson, an American who visited Paris in the 1830s said, "The French dine to gratify, we to appease the appetite. We demolish dinner, they eat it." And, "The French never showed the slightest sign of hurry or impatience. It was as if they had nothing else to do but sit and chatter and savor what seemed to Americans absurdly small portions." I believe this could just as easily be said today.

It is food that brings together friends and families after a long day at work or school. It is food that brings together friends and families to celebrate all the special occasions in our lives—weddings, christenings, birthdays, holidays, promotions. And today, nearly half of all business transactions, including job interviews are conducted at the table. If you are unfamiliar with formal table settings and how to properly eat the various courses, you may find the experience of dining with others stressful and unenjoyable.

The Art of Dining Well—Everything You Need to Know to Shine at the Table is a guide that will help you more thoroughly enjoy this centuries-old custom of sharing meals with others by giving you the knowledge and skills to have the confidence in knowing that you are doing the right thing at the table.

Does it really matter if we know how to properly hold a knife and fork? Do others care if we have good table manners? The answer is a resounding "Yes" to both questions. People do care, and most people would prefer to eat with someone who has some semblance of good table manners rather than someone who offends them with their lack of polished dining skills and distasteful table manners. After all, isn't it our civilized customs that separate us from the rest of the animal kingdom?

Young people who possess good table manners are always welcome at the table, whether at home, at school or in a restaurant. Children should be encouraged to practice their table manners just as they are encouraged to practice sports or musical instruments. And, whenever possible, parents should join their children for meals and conversation.

I always enjoy reading Munro Leaf's *Manners Can Be Fun* book to young students. It begins: "Having good manners is really just living with other people pleasantly. If you lived all by yourself on a dessert island, others would not care whether you had good manners or not." Most of us do not live on dessert islands; nor do most of us eat every meal alone; therefore, a sense of decorum at the table ensures that the shared experience of dining together is pleasant for everyone.

There is no better, or possibly worse place, for you to make an impression on others than at the dining table. A person's table manners are a good indication of his or her socioeconomic background and sensitivity to other people. Refinement in dining skills and table manners signals that a person is considerate of others and that he or she has been taught the necessary social graces to feel comfortable and confident when dining with others.

The good news, however, is that there is no socioeconomic barrier to learning how to properly conduct oneself at the dining table. And learning how to do so will not only take you further in your personal life, but it will also take you further in your professional life. Most cultures outside of the United States place a high value on this kind *savoir faire*.

As Mary Murphy Bosrock writes in her book, *Asian Business—Customs and Manners*, "How you eat and respond to food is essential for diplomacy. Your table manners can make or lose friends." Polished table manners will distinguish you from the crowd in business and social arenas worldwide.

From family meals at home to fine dining in a restaurant, *The Art of Dining Well—Everything You Need to Know to Shine at the Table* will prepare you to dine with anyone, anywhere! It is a comprehensive, step-by-step guide that will teach you all you need to shine at the table. You will learn how to "read" table settings, how to properly hold your silverware for each of the courses, how to eat difficult foods, how to graciously toast your host, and much more of the finer points of dining skills and table manners.

Are you ready to take your dining skills and table manners to the next level? Let's get started!

1

Table Settings and How to Read Them

The most important thing to remember is that the utensils we use are just tools and not objects of mystery. Elaborate table settings are less about good manners and more about etiquette.
- Bethanne Patrick, An Uncommon History of Common Courtesy

*A*t first glance, a formal table setting can be intimidating because there are so many forks, spoons, and knives, all for different courses. However, do not be intimidated; there is a simple system behind it all. The table is set with all the silverware that will be needed for the various courses that will be served, and it is arranged in order of their use. Not only does it make the service flow more smoothly to have the table laid with all that will be needed for the meal, but it also makes for an aesthetically pleasing sight to see a fully laid table—especially if care has been taken to the way it is presented.

Start with outermost fork or spoon in the place setting and work your way inward with each subsequent course. For example, if the salad will be served before the entrée, the salad fork will be the outermost fork on your left. If it will be served after the entrée, it will be to the immediate left of your plate.

Did you know?

The modern-day table setting is attributed to Charles I of England who in 1633 declared, "It is decent to use a fork," a statement that heralded the beginning of civilized table manners. It wasn't until a century later, however, that the fork gained acceptance among the lower class.

Formal Six-Course Continental Place Setting

Table Settings

- **Forks** are placed to the left of the service plate. **Knives** are placed to the right of it. Generally speaking. every fork is married to a knife. This means that for every fork on the left side of the plate, there will be a corresponding knife placed on the right side of it. One exception to this is the oyster or seafood fork, which will be on the right next to the soup spoon.

- **The soup spoon** is placed at the far right of the place setting—outside of the knives.

- **Salad fork:** Salad may be served before or after the main course. The placement of the salad fork at your place setting will let you know when it will be served. It is customary for the salad to be served after the main course outside of the United States.

- **Glasses** are always placed on the right side, above the dinner plate in the order they will be used—going from the outside in.

- **The bread plate** is placed on the left side above the dinner plate. A tip for remembering the placement of the bread plate and drinks it to make a "b" with your left index finger and thumb, and a "d" with your right index finger and thumb. Always, however, do this below the table.

- **A butter knife** will be located near the butter dish. Use it to transfer butter to your bread plate. Your butter knife will either be lying diagonally across your bread plate or as the last one to your right in the row of knives. Never use the knife with the butter dish to butter your bread. If there is no knife with the butter dish, transfer the butter with your butter knife to your plate.

- **The dessert fork and spoon** are placed horizontally above the plate, with the spoon above the fork. When dessert is served, slide them down to the sides of the dessert plate: fork on the left; spoon on the right.

- **Coffee spoons** are either to the right of the plate, above the dessert fork and spoon or brought with the coffee.

- **The order of the wine glasses** begins with the one furthest away from you on your right side: (a) Sherry (soup course) (b) White wine (fish/chicken course) (c) Red wine (meat course) (d) Water goblet. (There may be other glasses used throughout the meal.)

- **Finger bowls** are most often presented after the main course and before dessert. If the bowl is placed on a plate directly in front of you, lift the bowl with both hands and place it to the left of your place setting. If there is a doily under it, move it as well. Often the finger bowl will be placed to the left. Dip the fingers of one hand into the bowl, dry on your napkin which remains on your lap. Follow with the other hand. If there is a flower or a lemon slice in the bowl, leave it there.

Did You Know?

The first and only utensil was the dagger, the same threatening symbol of violence that you carried with you for defense. So, there are some serious restrictions regarding the knives at the table. The knife is never pointed at anyone. A blade pointed outward is a sign that you wish the person harm.

2

Taking a Seat, Conversation, and Posture at the Table

Keep all uncooked joints off the table.
-Mae West

Taking a Seat

- At formal dinner parties or business meals, if there are no place cards, the host or hostess will direct the guests where to take a seat.

- After your host has instructed you where he/she would like for you to sit, take your seat. As a general rule, the hostess will place the most honored male guest on her right and his partner on her husband's right. The next most honored guests would sit on her and her husband's left.

- To seat yourself, approach the right side of the chair and enter it from your left side.

- At a formal dinner party, tradition dictates a gentleman to help the lady on his right take her seat. The man to the hostess's left would seat her. Then, the other men at the table would take their seats.

- At a business meal, a lady does not expect a gentleman to pull out the chair for her. If he does, however, she should graciously accept his assistance.

Did You Know?

In Ancient Rome, hosts—and most honored guests—reclined on raised and cushioned platforms and ate by propping themselves on one elbow so they could reach food and drinks on a smaller platform set in front of them.

Conversation at the Table

- At one time, it was the custom for the gentleman, after taking his seat, to turn directly to the lady on his right and start talking. Then, after a while, he would turn to the lady on his left and talk to her. This custom called "turning the tables" was practiced at formal dinner parties where guests would watch the hostess to see when she stopped talking to the person on her right and began talking to the person on her left; when she did, everyone would follow her lead and turn to the person on their left. Now, we simply let common courtesy guide us. We know it is polite to talk to each person we are seated by, and once a conversation has ended, to turn from one person to the other person when it seems natural to do so.

- What is acceptable conversation at the dining table? As Somerset Maugham once said, "At a dinner party one should eat wisely, but not too well and talk well, but not too wisely." Pleasant, non-controversial topics, such as current events, cultural activities, and vacations are the best conversation topics for most dining occasions.

THE FINER POINTS:

* If there is a seating plan, be respectful of your host and sit in your designated seat. It is rude to change place cards.

* If you are meeting the person seated next to you for the first time, rather than beginning with the rather graceless "What do you do?" you might ask "How do you spend your days?" "Did you enjoy your day?" "What's been the best thing about your day?"

* Rather than asking, "Where are you from?" you might try the queen of England's classic line, "Have you come far?"

* Guests should wait until the host or hostess lifts his or her fork before eating.

* Do not ignore a person sitting beside you because he or she is uninteresting to you.

* Do not raise your voice to talk to people sitting a few seats down from you, but it is acceptable to include those sitting within close proximity to you.

* Do not discuss politics, religion, money, or any other topic that you think might cause unpleasantness.

* Do not discuss your food likes and dislikes, or your diet habits.

* Eat or talk; do not do both at the same time.

Posture at the Table and Placement of Hands

- Sit at a comfortable distance away from the table, so that when the elbows are bent the hands are level with the knives and forks, which should be an inch or two above the plate when preparing to use them.

- Sit erect and maintain good posture throughout the meal. Depending upon the chair, you may sit against the back of the chair if you do not look like you are slouching. Avoid crossing your legs. Keep both feet flat on the floor.

- Keep elbows close to your sides when eating. Move them forward and backward to convey food to the mouth and to manipulate the cutlery. They should not go "up-and-out" at your sides when you are cutting your food.

- In the American and English style, rest both hands on the lap when you are not eating.

- In the Continental style, rest the hands on the table from the wrists up when you are not eating.

Did You Know?

Forks were originally used for spearing rather than lifting or scooping, and for this reason usually had just two tines, set widely apart. Between the 17th and 18th century the tines increased from two to three, then to four.

THE FINER POINTS:

* Do not push back your chair and cross your legs away from the table until after dessert is finished. It is acceptable to do this if people are talking at the end of the meal, but not while people are still eating.

* Do not support yourself with your elbows resting on the table at any time during the meal when you are at a formal dinner party, or when you are dining in a formal restaurant.

* It is acceptable to rest an elbow or two on the table between courses and to lean in to hear what the person across from you is saying if you are in a casual restaurant and there is no food on the table.

Excusing Yourself from the Table

- If you need to excuse yourself to go to the restroom, place your napkin on the chair, push your chair in and say, "Please excuse me." It is not necessary to say where you are going.

- In the English style of dining, place your napkin on the table to the left side of your plate when you excuse yourself from the table.

- If possible, try to wait to excuse yourself to go to the restroom between courses.

- If you need to make an urgent phone call, excuse yourself from the table to take the call.

THE FINER POINTS:

* In many cultures, nose-blowing at the table is offensive. It is a bodily function and should be done away from the table. In an emergency, however, if there isn't time to excuse yourself to go the restroom, you may discreetly wipe your nose using a tissue or handkerchief, not your napkin.

Did you know?

Napkins are a relatively recent development. In the Middle Ages, people wiped their mouths on the tablecloth.

3

The Napkin: The Silent Signal

An elegantly folded napkin is a harbinger of good things to come, the invitation to a wonderful epicurean adventure, the promise of thoughtfulness and whimsy. It signals a celebration.
- David Stark, *Napkins with a Twist*

The napkin is one of the most significant items at your place setting. It is the "silent signal" that not only signals the beginning of the meal, but it also signals when the meal is over, and it is the host or hostess who is responsible for making these decisions. Of course, if it is an informal meal, the group will simultaneously place their napkins on their laps when everyone is seated, and then place them back on the table when everyone is finished with their meals.

The Napkin

- As soon as you sit down you should place the napkin on your lap. If there is a host or hostess, you would wait for him or her to place it on his or her lap first.

- Large dinner napkins remain folded in half with the fold closest to your body. Small luncheon napkins should be opened completely.

- Dinner napkins are usually 20" by 20,'" or larger. Luncheon napkins are smaller and are usually 16" by 16".

- A napkin is used by carefully dabbing the corners of your mouth, not wiping it. Touch your napkin lightly to your lips in the shape of an inverted "V" and dab once at each corner of your mouth, and then in the middle of your mouth.

- A napkin should be used to cover your mouth if you need to sneeze or cough. Turn your head toward your shoulder and cover your mouth and nose with your napkin before sneezing or coughing. Quietly say, "Please excuse me." Of course, if you need to blow your nose, you will need to excuse yourself from the table.

Did you know?

The idea of folding napkins derives from Italy, where animal shapes were popular in the 15th century. After the Restoration, it became fashionable in England to 'pinch' or fold napkins. An Englishman, Samuel Pepys, paid 40 shillings for his wife to be taught the art, having seen it at court.

- If you need to excuse yourself for any reason from the table during the meal, place the napkin on your chair, push the chair in, and simply say, "Excuse me." Always try to wait to excuse yourself between courses.

- When the meal is over and you are ready to leave the table, pull the napkin from the center through an opening between your thumb and forefinger and leave it to the left of your place setting. If there is a host or hostess, you would wait for him or her to do this first.

THE FINER POINTS:

* Do not unfold your napkin above the table; it should be done on your lap.

* Do not tuck your napkin in your collar, tie it around your neck, or stick it in your belt. If you eat your food correctly you won't need to worry about getting food on your clothes.

* Do not use your napkin to wipe your face, clean your utensils or eyeglasses, or blot your lipstick with it.

* Do dab gently at your mouth before taking a drink of your beverage to avoid leaving traces of food on your glass.

* Should you leave unsightly traces of food on your napkin, tuck that portion under so that it will not be seen when you bring it up to your mouth the next time.

* Do not wave your napkin in the air when you are talking.

* Never put your used napkin back on the table until the end of the meal when the host puts his or hers on the table. It would then be placed to the left of your place setting.

Did you know?

Egyptians, Greeks, and Romans used "serviettes," napkins, the size of bath towels.

4

Styles of Eating—American and Continental

Well-bred people are accustomed to using the right knife or fork at the right time, and their manners—or manner—at the table is characterized by a fine graciousness and ease that make others feel at ease, too.
-Lillian Eichler, *The New Book of Etiquette,* 1924

There are two standard styles of eating when using silverware: the American style and the Continental style. The American style, which is also referred to as the cut-and-switch or zig-zag style, is primarily used in North America. The Continental style, also known as the European style, is a global style that is used throughout the world.

The cut-and-switch style of dining is originally European and was adopted by nineteenth-century Americans from France—the "arbiter of elegance"—for them then. But in the mid-nineteenth century, a French text claimed it was trendy to *not* cut-and-switch. Americans, however, did not change their style of eating, and to this day eat in what we refer to as the American style of eating or the cut-and-switch style.

You many dine in whichever style you are comfortable, as long as you do it correctly and maintain the same style throughout the meal. The global Continental style, however, is more graceful, efficient, and quieter, and is the recommended style for those who regularly travel outside of the United States for business.

The American Style: How to Properly Hold and Use Your Knife and Fork

The world was my oyster, but I used the wrong fork.
-Oscar Wilde

- The American style of eating is a four-step motion. First, the meat is cut; then the knife is placed on the upper right rim of the plate; the fork is switched to the right hand, and then the food is conveyed to the mouth with the tines upward.

- The knife and fork are held in the same manner in the hands for the two styles of eating.

Did you know?

In France in the 1630s, Richelieu, chief minister to Louis XIII got tired of watching people stabbing their knives and daggers into chunks of food and then at the end of the meal picking their teeth with the sharp end of the daggers. He ordered the kitchen staff to file off the sharp points of all house knives, and soon rounded knives became the latest thing.

How to Hold the Knife and Fork

- Take your knife in your dominant hand, blade down, and cup the handle in your palm of your hand. Place your index finger on top of the back of the blade, right where it attaches to the handle.

- Take the fork in the other hand, with the tines facing down. Cup the handle in the palm of your left hand and place your index finger on top of the back of the handle, pointing toward the tines.

Cutting Position: American and Continental

- Use your dominant hand when cutting your meat, which should be cut one bite at a time.

- When cutting, keep your elbow slightly above the table level and close to your sides.

- Use your fork to spear the meat and steady it so that it stays in place on the plate when you are cutting.

- After cutting the meat, place the knife on the upper right rim of the plate with the cutting edge of the blade facing the center of the plate.

- Switch the fork to your right hand before raising it to your mouth, tines upward.

- The fork is held like a pencil with the thumb and the second and third fingers. The fourth and fifth fingers rest in the hand. The index finger extends along the back of the fork for leverage, not putting it too close to the tines.

Resting Position: American Style

- When taking a pause from eating, or resting, the fork is laid on the plate in the resting position, slightly below the knife with the tines facing upward.

- The way you place your silverware on your plate in both the resting and finished positions is called the "silent service code," since it silently signals to the wait staff that you are either resting or finished with your course.

Finished Position: American Style

- When you have finished eating, the fork and knife are placed together diagonally on the plate in the finished position. They are laid with the handles in the four o'clock position on the right rim of the plate. The tips rest in the ten o'clock position.

- In the resting and finished positions, the blade of the knife is always laid on the plate with the blade of the knife facing inward.

- For left-handed persons, the placement on the plate in the resting and finished positions is the mirror-image of the placement for right-handed persons.

THE FINER POINTS:

* Do not hold the fork up in the left hand with prongs up and pile food on it with the knife.

* Do not use your fork to stab your food.

* Do not hold the knife in the left hand—unless, of course, you are left-handed.

* Do not place the knife and fork like a pair of oars in a rowboat, hanging off the plate's edge.

* Do take a break from eating after every few bites to converse with your dining companions.

* Do not wave your knife in the fork in the air to aid in your conversation.

* Do not place your fork and knife, or any utensil, back on the table after you have used it.

The Continental Style: How to Properly Hold and Use Your Knife and Fork

The way you cut your meat reflects the way you live.
-Confucius

- The Continental style is also referred to as the European style.

- It is a two-step motion.

- The way in which the knife and fork are held and cutting position is the same as the American style.

- Your knife and fork do not change hands in the Continental style. The knife remains in your right hand if your fork is in your left hand. They work together as a team.

- Food must be balanced on the back of the rounded tines before conveying it to your mouth, which is done by slightly twisting your wrist when you bring the food to your mouth and eating off the back of the tines.

Cutting Position: American and Continental

- Cut only one piece of meat at a time.

- Use your fork to spear the meat and steady it so that it stays in place on the plate when you are cutting. Always cut behind the fork, never in front of it.

- To secure the meat on the tines of the fork, use the knife as a pusher, pushing the meat onto the tines. You may add a little of whatever accompanies the meat to the fork in the same bite.

- If you occasionally want to eat some vegetables with your right hand, lay your knife on the side of the plate with the sharp edge of the blade facing inward toward the plate. Do not, however in the Continental style shift the fork back and forth every time you cut a piece of meat.

- If the meat or fish does not need to be cut with the knife, it may be eaten with the fork in the right hand with the tines up. When you are finished, place the knife on the plate along with the fork—tines up—in the 10:20 o'clock finished position.

- When dining in the Continental style, both knife and fork are picked up to eat at the same time and both are put down to rest at the same time.

- When you would like to take a sip of your beverage or engage in conversation, place your knife and fork in the resting position with the fork, tines down, placed over the knife--the blade facing in—in an inverted "V" position.

Resting Position-Continental Style

- If there is room on your plate when you would like to rest, lay your knife and fork on the plate near the center in an inverted "V" position, as pictured above. If there is too much food on your plate to do this, simply lay your fork on the left side of the plate and your knife on the right side, slightly angled so that the tips are facing each other.

Finished Position: Continental

- When you have finished eating, place your knife and fork side by side diagonally on your plate in the finished position. The handles are laid in the four o'clock position on the right rim of the plate. The tips rest in the ten o'clock position. The tines of the fork will be placed downward.

- In Great Britain, the knife and fork are placed side-by-side in the 6 o'clock position to indicate you are finished with your meal. In Europe, the knife and fork are placed in the 3:15 position.

THE FINER POINTS:

* Do not hold the fork in the left hand with the prongs up and pile food on it with the knife.

* Do not eat with the fork in the left hand—tines down—without holding the knife in the right hand.

* Do not hold the knife in the left hand unless you are left-handed.

* Always place your knife on your plate with the blade facing inward.

* Do not place the knife and fork like a pair of oars in a rowboat half on the plate and half off when you are resting.

* The way in which your utensils are laid on the plate in both the American and Continental styles silently "tells" the wait staff whether we are resting or finished with a course. This is called the silent service code.

Did you know?

The custom of laying the knife down with the blade facing inward dates back to the Middle Ages when an inward-facing blade indicated goodwill, as opposed to an outward-facing blade ready for retaliation against the enemy.

5

Forms of Service: Dinner is Served!

At Windsor Castle, notes for the footman on duty traditionally recorded: Trays must be kept level so that there is no spilling of gravy or sauces—do not attempt to hurry when carrying a loaded tray.
-Kathryn Jones, *For the Royal Table: Dining at the Palace*

There are three traditional ways of serving the fish and main courses: service à la française, or French; service à la russe or Russian style; and service à l'anglaise. A fourth, less formal form of service, which is primarily used in the Unites States, is called the service American style.

1. **Service à la française.** The French style of service is standard at formal meals. A server presents an arranged platter of food to each guest on his left side. The guest then serves himself or herself with the fork and serving spoon on the platter. He or she then places the serving utensils side by side back on the platter with the spoon on the right, bowl up, and the fork on the left, tines down.

2. **Service à l'anglaise.** In the English style of service, a server presents an arranged platter of food from the left and then serves each guest, rather than having them serve themselves. This style of service is generally used when there are large numbers of guests because it allows the server to limit the size of the portions served to a predetermined number of guests.

3. **Service à la russe.** This Russian style of service is most often observed in upscale restaurants. A server presents a decorated platter of meat, fish, or poultry to the table and then carves it at the sideboard in front of the guests. In a restaurant, the food is cooked and carved on a rolling table, which is usually equipped with a side burner.

4. **Service American style.** This form of service is the fastest and most casual way of serving food; it does not require professional service. The food is placed directly on the guest's plate in the kitchen and then brought out and placed at each person's place at the table. This is the most common style used for family dinners.

Did you know?

In the 19th Century the service à la française was gradually replaced by one in which each course was served singly in succession. This system, known as service à la russe after Prince Kourakine, the Ambassador of Tsar Alexander I, who seems to have introduced it in France. This style of service meant that the courses remained hotter and that there was far more space on the table, but a larger quantity of glass and cutlery and more labor were required. Food and drink are now served by the staff.

Buffet Lunches and Dinners

Although informal by their very nature, buffet lunches or dinners are appropriate for formal as well as informal occasions. They are perfect for hosting large groups when you do not have a lot of help or a large enough table at which to seat everyone.

There are two types of buffets: the classic buffet, at which guests sit away from a dining room table; and the seated buffet, at which guests serve themselves and then sit at a dining room table.

- When a line forms at the buffet table, take your place at the end of the line.

- Serve yourself a moderate amount; do not overload your plate.

- Do not eat while standing in the buffet line.

- For a classic buffet, you will take a seat wherever you can find one in the living room or wherever the buffet is being held. Spread your napkin on your lap before placing your plate on it.

- If there are not enough seats for everyone, the younger people should leave the chairs for the adults, or older men and women.

- At an informal buffet, you do not have to wait for all the guests at the table to be seated to eat. However, you should wait until at least a few guests have seated themselves at the table.

6

The Courses and How to Eat Them

Remember that a dinner party is not a funeral nor has your hostess invited you because she thinks you are in dire need of food. You are there to be entertaining. Be gay. Do your part.
-Walter Hoving, *Tiffany's Table Manners for Teenagers*

Formal Six-Course Place Setting

The Courses: American or Continental Style

Three courses are customary for most informal dinner parties and when we are dining out, but the number of courses for a meal can vary from one to as many as ten or twelve courses, although it is quite rare to have more than five or six courses at even the most formal dinner parties now.

A formal eight-course dinner would include: an appetizer, soup, sorbet, a fish course, a meat course, salad, dessert, and coffee. Today, six courses are the maximum for even the most formal dinner parties. A four-course meal would normally include a salad, soup, main course, and dessert.

Did You Know?

For centuries after individual use of knives and forks became common, people carried their own from place to place. It is thought that the reason Europeans shifted their eating style—eating with their forks in their left hands—was due to the Colonials "aping" the Old Country's table manners. Continental types switched their forks from their right to the left.

Four-Course Place Setting

Six-Course Formal Dinner

1ˢᵗ Course: Soup

- The soup spoon is held by resting the end of the handle on your middle finger, with your thumb across the top.

- When eating soup, the spoon should be dipped away from you, not toward you. An exception to this rule is when eating onion soup: because of the cheese coating on the top, the soup spoon cuts into the crust with the spoon coming toward you.

- As an extra precaution to avoid getting soup on you, skim the bowl of the soup spoon along the edge of the soup bowl before bringing it up to your mouth.

- When you are served soup in a cup, with bits of meat, vegetables or croutons in it, eat the soup until all the food has been consumed. Then, you may pick up the soup and sip it directly from the cup.

- Never blow on your soup. You must wait for it to cool.

- Put only a modest amount of soup on your spoon, and quietly sip it from the side of the spoon.

- When most of the soup is eaten, you may tip the bowl away from you to get the last of the soup.

Did You Know?

Spoons date back to 5000 B.C.; metal knives, from about 2000 B.C.; but forks weren't commonly seen until A.D. 800.

*"Like tiny ships cast out to sea,
I dip the soup away from me."*

- Place the spoon in the bowl when you are taking a pause from eating.

- When you are finished, place your soup spoon on the service plate under the bowl in the 10:20 finished position.

- For a formal dinner, sherry would be served with soup. This will be the smallest stemmed glass on the farthest right of your glasses.

Finished Position

2nd Course: Fish

- The fish knife is used to break the fish and push it onto the fork.

- The fish knife is held differently than the dinner knife because the fish is not actually cut; it is simply broken apart. It is held the way you would hold a pencil.

- The fork should be held in the left hand with the tines down when you are cutting.

Cutting Position for the Fish Knife and Fish Fork

- When the fish is soft and boneless and does not need to be cut, you may simply use your fork—held in the right hand with the tines up—and leave your knife on the table. When you are resting, place your fork down along the right side of the plate.

- Fishbones are removed with the thumb and index finger and placed on the side of the plate.

- When you have finished eating, place the fish fork and knife together on the plate in the 10:20 o'clock finished position with the tines of the fork up.

- For the fish course, white wine is generally served.

3rd Course: Sorbet

- Although sorbet was once served between every course to clear the palate of the distinctive flavors of each course, it is now only served between the fish and the main course.

- Sorbet is served with its own spoon on the underlying plate. The spoon used to eat it will not be at the place setting before the meal.

- Sorbet is eaten as you would eat ice cream.

- The spoon is placed on the underlying plate when you are finished.

Did you know?

The serving of "ices" dates back to the Roman Empire when packed snow was brought down from the mountains; the emergence of sorbetto was not seen until the middle of the 16th century in Italy.

4th Course: Main Course

- The main, or meat course, may be eaten in either the American or Continental style, using the main course knife and fork, which is the largest knife and fork at your place setting.

Cutting Position for American and Continental Styles

- If there is a sauce left on the plate you would like to eat, spear a small piece of bread or roll with your fork, and then squish the bread around with your fork in the last bit of sauce and eat it.

- Should your main course not require a knife, leave the knife on the table until you have finished, and then pick it up and place it on the plate with your fork in the 10:20 finished position so the wait staff will know you are finished with this course.

- If red meat is served for the main course, you will be served an accompanying red wine with it. This will be the stemmed glass with the largest bowl to the right of the water glass. If you are served chicken for your main course, you will be served an accompanying white wine with it. This will be the stemmed glass with the smallest bowl to the right of your water glass.

5th Course: Salad

- The salad course may be eaten with the salad knife and fork; or, if you prefer to eat your salad with a salad fork alone, the knife may be left on the table until you have finished.

- If you eat with your salad fork alone, it must be held in your right hands, tines up.

- If the salad fork is used alone, use the fork to fold the lettuce into a convenient size rather than cutting it into small pieces.

- When cheese is served with the salad, use the cheese server on the platter and place a small portion of cheese on your salad plate, along with crackers or bread.

- Use your salad knife to put cheese on crackers or bread.

- Place the knife and fork in the 10:20 finished position on your salad plate when you are finished, even if you have only used the fork.

6*th* Course: Dessert

- Pie or cake a la mode and berries or any cup-fruit is eaten is with a fork and spoon. It is more easily eaten Continental style with the spoon in your right hand and the fork in your left hand.

- When eating dessert with a spoon and fork, the fork should be held in the left hand, tines down, and the spoon in the right. The fork holds the pie or cake in place, while the spoon is used to cut it. Then the fork pushes it, along with the ice cream, onto the spoon, and it is eaten with the spoon.

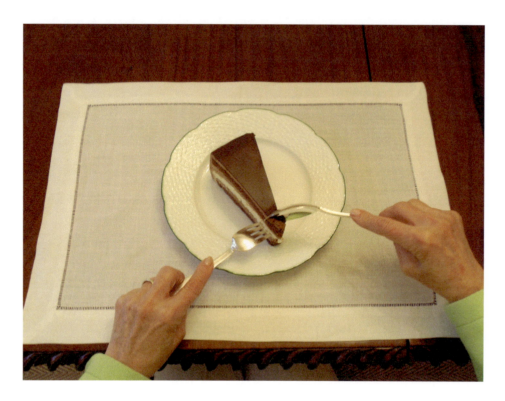

Cutting Position

- When they are served separately, eat pie or cake with a fork, and ice cream or pudding with a spoon.

- If fresh fruit is served, another piece of silverware will be provided for it.

Resting Position

- Lay the fork tines down on the left side of your plate, and the spoon up on the right side of it, as pictured above.

Finished Position

- When you have finished, place the fork and spoon in the 10:20 finished position on the plate with the fork placed prongs down and the bowl of the spoon up.

Finger Bowls

- The finger bowl is often seen at formally-served dinners. A server will bring you the finger bowl just before dessert is served.

- The server will place your finger bowl on a dainty doily in the center of your dessert plate with the dessert spoon balanced on the right side of the plate and the fork balanced on the left side. The finger bowl will be filled with cold water and possibly a lemon slice.

- Gently dip the fingers of each hand separately into the water and then dry them on your napkin below the top of the table.

- Now lift the doily, together with the finger bowl, and place them at the upper left of your place setting.

- Then move the fork and spoon from the plate to the left and right sides of the plate. Your empty plate is now ready for your dessert.

Coffee

- Demitasse, or coffee in a regular-sized cup, may be offered with dessert or after dessert with chocolate candies.

- The coffee cup handle is held with the thumb and the index finger or first two fingers and the fourth and fifth fingers are curled inward toward the palm.

- Coffee is usually served after dessert has been placed on the table. Coffee is considered a separate course if it is served after the dessert course is finished. In Europe, it is generally served after the dessert plate has been removed from the table. For classical formal dinners, coffee is served away from the table after dessert.

- A teaspoon is placed on the table during the coffee service, or on occasion, it is placed on the table between the knife and soup spoon.

- Try not to overfill your cup with coffee or cream; and avoid swirling it around too much, making a splash and puddle in your saucer.

- If you are given packets of sugar for your coffee, make sure to fold the packets once you have used them and place them under your saucer.

- Do not slurp your coffee; sip it gently.

- If your coffee is too hot, wait for it to cool—don't blow on it.

- Do not leave your spoon in the cup; place it on your saucer.

Bread/Rolls and Butter

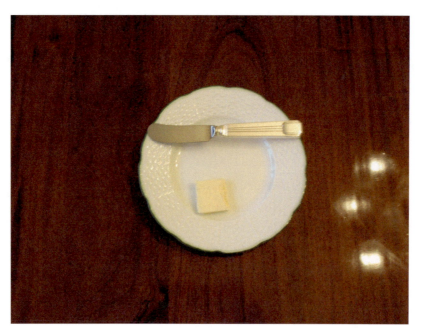

- Rolls are broken with your fingers.

- Break off one bite-size piece at a time, butter it, and eat it.

- Always break your bread over your bread plate, not the table.

- The butter knife is used only to cut the butter—never the roll.

- If no butter knife is set, use the "master" knife that is passed with the butter or your clean dinner knife.

- If a butter knife is not set, use your dinner knife, and then rest it on your bread or dinner plate.

- The bread plate may also be used for fish bones, olive pits, and other small items you may wish to remove from your mouth.

- When given olive oil instead of butter for your bread, pour a little on your bread plate. If you are not given a bread plate, be sure to follow the "no double-dipping" rule if you must share the olive oil with your dinner companions.

- Bread such as a pastry or dry toast is cut in half or quartered.

- Toast may be buttered entirely, or the end is buttered one bite at a time.

Did you know?

The practice of not biting into whole pieces of bread dates back to medieval times when leftovers were handed down to diners at lower tables. Tearing off pieces instead of biting directly into the bread was deemed more considerate of those to whom the bread would be "handed down."

7

The Asian Style of Eating—Eating with Chopsticks

Marriage is like twirling a baton, turning handsprings, or eating with chopsticks. It looks easy until you try it.
-Helen Rowland, American Journalist, 1875 - 1950

China, Japan, Korea, and Vietnam have had chopsticks as part of their traditional eating utensils for thousands of years. The Chinese use chopsticks because they consider the cutting of food at the table crude and barbaric. They believe all carving should be done in the kitchen, and that food is brought to the table in small enough pieces to be conveyed easily to the mouth with the use of chopsticks.

How to Use Chopsticks

Step One

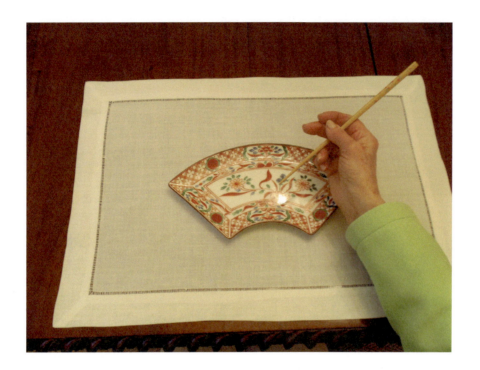

Step One

- The chopsticks will be held in your dominant hand.

- Pick up the first chopstick and place it between your middle finger and the base of your thumb. This one is your anchor; it should not move. Stiffen your hand for a firm grip. Have the broad end of the chopstick lay in the crook of your hand, where your thumb and pointer finger connect. Rest the narrow end between the base of your thumb and the side of your index finger. It is similar to how you hold a pen, but a bit lower.

Step Two

Step Two

- Grip the second chopstick with your index finger and thumb. This is the stick that moves. Place your thumb over the side of the second chopstick, so it rests above the first. Adjust your grip to a more comfortable position. Make sure the narrow tips of the chopsticks are even with each other to help prevent them from crossing or being unable to "pinch" the food.

Step Three

Step Three

- Keep the lower chopstick in its original position and move the upper chopstick with your thumb, index finger, and middle finger to pick up the food.

- The lower chopstick serves as a base for the food after it has been picked up by the upper chopstick.

- Then, the food will be conveyed to your mouth by the two chopsticks.

Did You Know?

Although chopsticks were created around 5,000 years ago in China to use for cooking, it wasn't until the Chinese philosopher Confucius (551-479 BC), who advocated their use for eating due to his disdain for knives at the table, that chopsticks became the preferred eating utensil in China. Confucius equated knives with acts of aggression, which went against his teachings. Chopsticks, on the other hand, reflect gentleness and benevolence.

General Dining Guidelines

- Never begin to eat or drink before your host or hostess does.

- It is very rude in any Asian restaurant to rub wooden or bamboo chopsticks together because that indicates you think the utensils are cheap.

- Use the large ends of your chopsticks to serve yourself from a platter.

- Never eat food directly from a platter—always place the food on your plate first.

- Never stand chopsticks in a bowl of rice.

- Never jam your chopsticks vertically into your food.

- Never point your chopsticks at someone.

- Do not cross the chopsticks. When not in use, place the chopsticks side-by-side on the chopsticks' holder.

- When eating rice, it is customary to hold the bowl close to your mouth.

- It is considered polite to sample every dish.

- Never take the last bit of food from a serving dish.

- If you do not want refills of tea, leave some in your cup.

- The serving of fruit signals the end of the meal.

Did you know?

From ancient times until the mid-19th century, rice was used as currency for paying taxes and wages. Like the rank of feudal lords, who were all measured by how much rice they had, rice indicated one's economic status.

8

Stemware, Beverages, and Toasts

*Wine makes every meal an occasion, every table more elegant,
every day more civilized.*
- Andre Simon, Author and Wine Merchant, 1877- 1970

Stemware

The table is set with the stemware for the beverages that will be served for a meal in the same manner as the dining utensils—in the order in which they will be used, going from the outside in.

At the minimum, every table should be set with a glass for water. It will be the glass that is laid at one o'clock above the dinner knife and the glass furthest left in the grouping of glasses.

No more than four glasses are generally set on the table: water, white wine, red wine, and champagne. A fifth glass—the sherry glass—is rarely seen today.

Front: Water, White Wine, Sherry.
Back: Champagne, Red Wine.

Generally speaking, all stemware should be held by the stem, although some say stemware that holds red wine may be held by the bowl. If, however, you are a child or an adult who is concerned about your glass tipping over, it is perfectly fine to hold your glass by the bowl at the table—better that than on the table.

Did You Know?

In King Tut's Egypt—around 1300 BC—the commoners drank beer and the upper class drank wine.

Beverages

Whether dining at home or in a restaurant, water should always be served. Whatever else one chooses to drink is a personal choice—whether it is wine, beer, coke, or milk, as long as it is drunk out of a glass when at the table. Of course, at a formal dinner party, it will be up to the host or hostess to choose the beverages that complement the meal. More than likely wine will be selected and possibly champagne for toasting.

THE FINER POINTS:

* If wine is being served in a restaurant or at someone's home, and you do not wish to have any, simply place your fingertips lightly on the rim of the glass when the server approaches to pour. Do not turn your glass upside down. Say, "I'm not having any today (or this evening)." That sends the message that you don't disapprove of wine, and others should feel no compunction about enjoying their wine.

* When you are hosting a business meal with a client, always ask "Would you like a beverage?" rather than asking "Would you like a drink?" A beverage can be alcoholic or non-alcoholic.

* Never order more than one or two glasses of wine if you are dining with a client who is not ordering an alcoholic beverage.

Wine Etiquette in a Restaurant

> *"Good wine is a familiar creature if it be used well."*
> -Shakespeare, *Othello*

Wine etiquette in a restaurant can be a seemingly difficult ordeal, but it doesn't have to be. When choosing a wine from a restaurant's wine list, the main goal is to achieve a suitable pairing with the entrees of your party. If the food orders are too different to generalize, you may want to consider ordering splits or order by the glass.

Waiters and sommeliers are there to answer your questions, so don't hesitate to ask them. No one knows the wine list or the food on the menu better than the people who work in the restaurant. It is the sommelier's job to design the wine list, to ensure that all of the items on the menu have wines that can be paired with them, and to help people find their way through the wine list.

It is your job to say:

- What you will be ordering from the menu to eat.

- How much you want to spend.

- What you have in mind.

- What sorts of wine you generally like—red, white, sweet, a little dry—whatever you can think of.

When the bottle of wine is presented to you at the table, you can do a quick check to make sure it is what you ordered. The cork may be placed on the table in front of you; don't worry about smelling the cork, unless it has a strong odor. The waiter or sommelier will then pour a little wine in your glass to see if it is okay with you before pouring it into your guests' glasses. Simply give the glass a little swirl, smell the wine, then taste it. It is perfectly acceptable to refuse a wine that has gone bad, but it is not acceptable to send a wine back because you don't like how it tastes.

After you, the host or hostess, have taken a sip and given your approval, the waiter will move on to the next person and fill everyone's glasses half full, coming back to you last. As a guest, you should wait to take a drink until your host or hostess has done so.

Did you know?

Although Dom Perignon, a French monk (1638-1715) has been credited with being the one who invented champagne, it isn't true. In fact, the English, rather than the French were the ones who invented champagne; or certainly the first reference—1676—was made by Englishman Sir George Etheredge of "sparkling" wine. The first French documents that refer to champagne date from 1748. History does, however, concede that Dom Perignon made significant contributions to the development of champagne, from vine management to cellar techniques.

Toasting Etiquette

Come quickly, I am drinking the stars.
-Dom Perignon

Toasts are always appropriate to acknowledge an occasion, welcome a new colleague, launch a new business, welcome an important visitor, or to simply add an element of festivity to a dinner party. A toast is a compliment and acknowledgment of the event and guests.

Champagne has always been the traditional beverage used for toasting at formal occasions, but it is now considered perfectly acceptable to toast with a non-alcoholic beverage.

- The perfect toast is short, funny, and heartfelt. The perfect length is three minutes.

- The protocol for toasting dictates that the host should give the first toast.

- There are two times during a formal meal when it is appropriate to propose a toast: the first toast is the welcome toast made by the host, and the second toast is made during the dessert course to honor the guest of honor if there is one.

- When the host proposes a toast to the guest of honor, he stands, turns to the person being toasted, looks him in the eye, and raises his glass to him. The other guests at the table follow suit and everyone drinks except the person being toasted. (Never drink to yourself.)

- After receiving a toast, the guest of honor should rise and propose a toast to the host.

Did you know?

In 16th century England, water was too dangerous to drink, and Queen Elizabeth I had beer or wine with breakfast. Even wine could be tainted, and the favorite remedy was to float a piece of spiced bread in the cup to improve the flavor, as well as provide a bit of nourishment. Raising the glass eventually came to be named for the bread: a toast.

9

Patricia's Rules for the Table

The last gasp of ceremony in our lives, the last ceremonial act in the twentieth century, is to sit down and dine. And to do it well, you have to bring passion to this small moment in time. Dining well is a gesture that should elevate us.
-John Saladino, *Designer*

As Emily Post once said, "The real test of table manners is never to offend the sensibilities of others." Good table manners are really nothing more than having a sensitive awareness of others and conducting oneself in a manner that makes the dining experience pleasant for everyone involved. Some of the rules for the table were devised for the safety of the diner, and others to make the act of eating more attractive. The best table manners are unaffected and natural, making those around you feel comfortable. Of course, mastering the art of the meal, fine dining skills, and good table manners may take practice, but once you have mastered this art, you will have the grace and refinement to dine with anyone, anywhere in the world.

By following the dining guidelines outlined on the previous pages and observing the rules for the table listed below you will be sure to shine at the table.

Patricia's Top 20 Rules for the Table

1. Wait until everyone has been served to begin eating— unless your host says you do not need to wait, or you are with a large party.

2. Avoid talking with food in your mouth.

3. Chew your food quietly with your mouth closed.

4. Wait until you have swallowed the food in your mouth and dabbed your mouth with your napkin before you take a sip of your beverage.

5. Cut and eat one piece of meat at a time before cutting the next one.

6. Never lick your fingers. Wipe your fingers and mouth with your napkin.

7. Once you have taken a utensil off the table and used it, it should never touch the table again. Place it on your plate in either the resting or finished position.

8. Bring your food to your mouth when you eat; do not bend your head down to your food.

9. Do not reach over someone's plate for something; ask for the item to be passed.

10. Never reach over another person's plate and "spear" food out of it with your fork.

11. Pass food and other items to the right, or counterclockwise, at the table.

12. Always pass the salt and pepper together. They are "married" and never separated.

13. Use a utensil instead of your fingers unless you are eating "finger foods;" and never use your fingers to push food onto your spoon or fork; use your knife.

14. Avoid spreading your elbows when cutting. Keep them close to your sides.

15. Eat at a similar pace as the others at the table. Do not eat too quickly or too slowly.

16. Never pick food out of your teeth with your fingers or a toothpick at the table.

17. Never blow your nose on your napkin or at the table.

18. Do not place your cell phone, keys, glasses, or handbag on the table.

19. Do not answer your cell phone or text on it while you are at the table.

20. Always thank the host at the end of the meal.

Did you know?

Erasmus, Dutch humanist and author of the first book of manners in 1526, was among the first to be concerned about table manners. He insisted that diners never lick their fingers or wipe their hands on their coats. His advice included: it was better to wipe one's fingers on the tablecloth; wipe your spoon before passing it to a neighbor and do not blow your nose with the same hand that you use to hold the meat.

10

How to Eat Certain Foods

No man is lonely eating spaghetti, for it requires so much attention.
-Christopher Morley, American Journalist, 1890-1957

Finger Foods and Foods that May be Eaten with Your Hands

- Asparagus. If the asparagus is served cold and not covered with a sauce, it can be picked up and eaten with your fingers.

- Bacon. May be eaten with your fingers if it is crisp.

- Buffalo chicken wings and spareribs. Be sure to put your bones in a "bone bucket" or bowl.

- Caviar. Use the serving spoon to put some caviar on your plate, and your own knife or spoon to gently prepare your portion. Take care not to overload your cracker or toast point with the sieved chopped egg and caviar.

- Cherry tomato. This is a one-bite food.

- Cookies, cupcakes, and cake, if bite-size. Eaten with your fingers, accompanied by a napkin to catch any crumbs.

- Corn-on-the cob. Held tightly at the ends with your fingers. Butter and season several rows at a time, not the entire ear of corn.

- Dips and chips. Meant to be shared, which is why a considerate guest will not re-dip a chip that has already been in his or her mouth.

- French fries at a fast-food restaurant. May be picked up and eaten in two or three small bites.

- Fried chicken. May be eaten with your fingers if you are at a picnic or at home with your family.

- Hot dogs, hamburgers, lunch sandwiches. If large, cut your hamburger or sandwich in half before picking it up. Messy or open-faced sandwiches should be eaten with a knife and fork.

- Pizza. Hold the pizza with your fingers and curl the sides so that the topping doesn't slide.

- Radishes, celery, pickles, and olives. If passed at dinner, spoon them onto your bread or cocktail plate.

- Shrimp with the tail. When the shrimp comes with the tale on it, you may hold the tail with your fingers and dip it in the sauce. One dip and two bites are recommended.

- Sushi. May be eaten with your fingers or chopsticks. Sashimi is only to be eaten with chopsticks.

- **T**acos. Use your hands to start, then switch to your fork if it starts getting messy.

- **T**ea sandwiches and canapes. Are eaten with your fingers.

- **U**npeeled fruit. If eaten away from the table, may be eaten with your hands.

> ### *Did you Know?*
>
> *Asparagus was cultivated in gardens in ancient Rome as far back as the first century A.D. "As quick as asparagus" was an old Roman saying meaning something accomplished quickly. In the 1600s King Louis XIV of France had his gardeners grow asparagus in greenhouses so he could enjoy it year-round.*

How to Eat Certain Other Foods

- **A**rtichokes are served cooked and eaten with your fingers by pulling off one leaf at a time and dipping the pulpy base of each leaf into the sauce and then scraping it off the leaf with your teeth. When you get to the prickly part at the base of the artichoke scrape it off to uncover the heart. Use your knife and fork to eat the heart of the artichoke.

- **C**heese served as hors d'oeuvres are spread on crackers with a knife. When cheese and fruits are served for dessert, the cheese is cut and eaten with a fork. Runny cheeses such as Camembert and Brie are always spread crackers with a knife. Hard cheeses may be picked up with the fingers to eat. Never cut the tip off a wedge of cheese. Cut along the length, leaving the wedge in a similar shape.

- Clams, oysters, and mussels on the half-shell. Hold or steady the shell, if necessary, with one hand and remove the morsel whole with an oyster or cocktail fork. Dip it in butter or broth and eat it in one bite. Fried clams are eaten with a fork.

- Condiments. When helping yourself to condiments at the table, put each condiment on your plate beside the food, not directly on the food itself. Then, use your knife to put the condiment directly on your food. Butter or jam is put on the bread plate before putting it on your bread or roll.

- Lemon. When you use a lemon to season food, secure a wedge of it with your fork and use your hand to squeeze out the juice. Your hand should also act as a shield around the lemon when you squeeze it.

- Lobster. It is easiest to first tackle a lobster by twisting off the front claws. Crack the claws with a nutcracker and remove the meat with an oyster fork and or a nut pick. Next, break the tail off the body. Lift the meat out with a fork. Then, you can cut up the tail with a knife and fork. Then break off each leg and take the meat out with your oyster fork.

- Pasta comes in different sizes and shapes. For spaghetti, eat a few strands at a time, twirling them with your fork without a spoon; or if spaghetti is served with a spoon, hold the spoon in your left hand and twirl the spaghetti into a nest in the spoon. Do not, however, cut the strands of your spaghetti with your knife. You can eat small bite-sized pasta, such as ziti, penne or tortellini, with a fork.

- Potatoes. A baked potato served hot and is eaten with a fork. It is held in place with the fingers of one hand while the fork breaks it open in a crosswise or lengthwise piercing motion. It is pushed open with the fingers to let the steam escape, and the fork is used to season it with butter or whatever toppings you choose to put on it.

- Sauces. May be poured, spooned, or put on the plate beside your meat. Use your fork to dip one bite at a time into the sauce.

> ### *Did you know?*
>
> *In ancient Greece and Rome, pepper arriving by caravan from India was considered so valuable that it was preferred to money, which fluctuated widely in value. Rents were paid in peppercorns, as well as taxes, dowries, and even bribes.*

How to Eat Fruit

> *First-class fruits possess in themselves an all-powerful attraction to the admiring gaze of all who behold them, yet it cannot be denied that their beauty is still further enhanced when tastefully grouped in graceful pyramids upon rich services in old Sevres, Dresden or Chelsea china.*
> -Charles Francatelli, Master Cook to Queen Victoria

When eaten at the table:

- Apples and pears are quartered, cored, and eaten with your fingers.

- Apricots. Fresh apricots are eaten with your fingers. Place the stone on your plate.

- Bananas. In a more formal setting, the banana is entirely peeled, and the peel is placed on the side of the plate. Then, the fruit is sliced one bite at a time and eaten with a fork. In a casual setting, the banana can be peeled partially or completely, and a small section broken off and eaten with your fingers.

- **Berries.** When berries are served with the stems removed, they are generally served with cream and sugar and eaten with a spoon. If berries, such as strawberries, come with the stems on, they may be eaten with the fingers.

- **Cherries.** Fresh, raw cherries are eaten with your fingers.

- **Fruit cocktail** is eaten with a spoon.

- **Grapefruit.** When the grapefruit half is presented to you, it should have each section pre-cut so that all you need to do is slide out each one with your spoon and eat it. If the sections have not been precut, use a small knife or serrated edge grapefruit spoon to separate the sections from the skin.

- **Grapes.** When a large bowl of grapes is presented, break off a small cluster of grapes with your fingers and put them on your plate. Eat the grapes with your fingers one at a time.

- **Melons.** Sliced melon is eaten with a fork; melon served in balls is eaten with a spoon.

- **Oranges and tangerines.** First, remove the peel with a knife. Then pull it apart with your fingers in manageable sections before eating it. Discretely spit any seeds into the palm of your hand before transferring them to your plate.

- **Peaches and pears** are eaten with the skin or peeled. Peel first, then core the pear; remove the stone from the peach and then quarter it. Eat these fruits in small bites, since they are full of juices and can be a bit messy.

- **Pineapple** that is served peeled and sliced on a plate is eaten with a knife and fork. If it is cubed and served in a bowl, it should be eaten with a spoon.

- **Stewed fruit** is eaten with a spoon.

- Watermelon is only eaten at informal meals since it is too messy to be included at a formal dinner party. Nevertheless, it is a very popular fruit that is often included on the menu in the summertime. Slices of watermelon may be held on your hand to eat or they can be eaten with a fork. If cubed the watermelon should be eaten with a spoon. As with other fruits that contain seeds, discreetly spit any seeds into the palm of your hand and place them on the side of the plate.

Did you know?

The apple has grown for thousands of years. From the beginning, apples have been associated with many special qualities such as beauty, health, pleasure, and temptation. Apples were known to Greeks and Romans are mentioned in Greek mythology: Gaia, or Mother Earth, presented a tree with Golden Apples to Zeus and his bride Hera on their wedding day.

11

Entertaining at Home: Courteous Host and Gracious Guest

The most effective entertaining is that which reflects the personal style of the host.
- Charlotte Ford, *Book of Modern Manners*

Although the food, wine, service, and setting are the key ingredients for a successful dinner party or social function, just as important is an understanding on the part of the host that their guests need to feel special and welcome. In addition, the host is responsible for drawing out each guest and encouraging interesting and stimulating conversation.

Guests should also keep in mind that they have a part to play in ensuring the event will be successful by being agreeable and sociable. I advise my clients to go with this mindset: seek to entertain; not be entertained. Charming, delightful guests are always invited back.

Protocol for the Host

- Always greet guests at the door and make them feel welcome.

- Immediately take jackets and coats. You can hand them to another person to hang up or put in a room that has been designated for the coats.

- Take any gifts and follow the same procedure as the coats.

- Introduce arriving guests to friends standing in the area.

- Give arriving guests directions to food and drinks.

- After all the guests arrive, the host should circulate to make sure everyone has someone to talk to and is enjoying himself or herself.

- Assign someone to make sure there are enough food and drinks for everyone.

- If you do not have place cards, let guests know where you would like for them to sit at the dinner table   Place the guest of honor to your right at the table; and his or her spouse or companion to the right of your co-host.

- As the host, it is your duty to give the signal when to begin the meal by putting your napkin on your lap, and to give the "silent" signal that it is over by placing your napkin on the table.

> ### *Did you know?*
>
> *We can thank nineteenth-century Russia for the use of place cards and place settings. Service* **à la russe** *—in which the host lays out all the plates, cutlery, and glassware each guest will need during the meal—has stayed with us through the centuries.*

Protocol for the Guest

- Never arrive early for a dinner party but try not to be more than twenty minutes late.

- Always take a hostess gift if you are going to someone's home for dinner.

- If it is a large party and your host is not at the door, work your way through the crowd and say hello to your host.

- Don't hesitate to introduce yourself to others and shake hands with them.

- If you are talking to someone and a person unknown to the two of you walks up, introduce yourself, then introduce the person with whom you were speaking.

- If you spill something, let the host know immediately, and offer to help.

- If you break something let the host know and offer to pay for the damage.

- Do not bring a friend to the party unless you have checked with the host first.

- Be a gracious and engaging guest: Make polite conversation with your dining companions and the other guests at the party.

- Always thank the host before you leave, and send a thank-you note the next day.

12

Entertaining for Business: Host and Guest Protocol

Sharing a meal with clients allows us to learn more about our clients in one evening than we could with three meetings in a conference room.
-Michael Parlapiano, The Culinary Edge

*E*ntertaining current and potential clients at a restaurant is an excellent opportunity to create a memorable experience and a favorable impression of yourself and the company you represent. People do business with people they like and feel comfortable with, and what better way to build rapport with someone than sharing a meal with them. Keep in mind, however, there is no better or possibly worse place to make an impression than at the table. Many job opportunities have been lost, promotions denied, and business deals not closed because of bad table manners and lack of polish at the table. So, it is vitally important that you exhibit impeccable decorum at business meals if you want to make a favorable impression.

Host Protocol

- Start by selecting a restaurant with which you are familiar, and one you think your client will like. Knowing the restaurant and staff will ensure you get the best service and will make you feel more comfortable.

- Dress appropriately for the restaurant.

- Arrive early and select a table. Seating and table location are important considerations during business meals. Request a table away from the kitchen, restrooms, or entryway.

- Prior to sitting, determine where you would like to seat your guest. If there is more than one guest, the most important guest should be seated to the right of the host; the second most important guest is on the host's left unless there is a co-host. If so, the second most important guest would be seated to the co-host's right.

- Stand when guests arrive, shake hands, and let them know where you would like for them to sit; and introduce them to the other guests if they are unknown to them.

- Let your guests order first, but not before discussing the menu with them and agreeing on how many courses everyone will order. Ideally, everyone at the table should order the same number of courses.

- At a business lunch, one should opt for manageable dishes that require a knife and fork to eat. Practice good table manners while dining, remembering to swallow before speaking and chew with your lips closed. Pace yourself, so that you and your guests are finished at the same time.

- Offer your guest a beverage. If he or she chooses not to have an alcoholic beverage, it is acceptable for you to order one, although I would recommend ordering no more than one alcoholic beverage.

- Always let guests know the reason for your invitation. Is it to get to know them better, thank them for their business, or perhaps discuss a new business opportunity with them? People like knowing the reason for business invitations.

- Avoid getting down to business as soon as you sit down. Conversation during the early part of the meal should be about building rapport with guests. Serious business is saved for later in the meal after the entrée plates have been removed.

- The host pays the bill, which includes the gratuity. As the host, you are also responsible for your guest's coat check and valet parking tips as well.

- Signal the end of the meal by placing your napkin on the table and rising from your chair. This is called the "silent signal."

Did you know?

R.S.V.P or RSVP is an acronym for the French phrase *respondez s'il vous plait*, which translates to the formal "respond if you please." The French and English established the custom of using R.S.V.P. on their invitations in the late eighteenth century. Today, one often sees "regrets only" on invitations.

Guest Protocol

> *Your manners are always under examination, and by committees little suspected, awarding or denying very high prizes when you least think about it.*
> Ralph Waldo Emerson

- Be on time.

- Dress appropriately for the restaurant.

- Greet your host first, and introduce yourself to the other guests at the table.

- Do not sit down at the table until you are directed where to sit by the host.

- Do not touch anything at the table until your host puts his or her napkin in his or her lap.

- Follow your host's lead when ordering; and place your order in an expedient manner without asking too many questions about how the food is prepared or requesting too many substitutions.

- Never season your food before tasting it—particularly if it is an interview luncheon. It indicates a lack of judgment on your part.

- Be an appreciative, cooperative, and sociable guest.

- Avoid doing any personal grooming at the table. It is very unprofessional, as well as bad manners.

- When the meal is finished, shake hands with your host and thank him or her.

- Write a thank-you note as soon as you return to your office.

13

The Restaurant Staff: At Your Service

A well-run restaurant is like a winning baseball team. It makes the most of every crew members' talents and takes advantage of every split-second opportunity to speed up service.
-David Ogilvy, Advertising Executive

Well-trained restaurant staff can only do its job well-- making sure that everything goes smoothly and that your dining experience in their restaurant is enjoyable-- if you as a diner or restaurant patron do what is expected of you. It is your job to know whom to ask for what in a restaurant, and to give them the proper cues with either the "silent service code," your eye contact, or words when you would like service.

The food, the ambiance, the service, and being appreciated for our patronage are what make us favor one restaurant over another. When delicious food is served to us in a timely manner by agreeable and attentive wait staff in an attractive setting, it makes for a memorable dining experience and one we wish to repeat. All we need to do is know how to effectively communicate our needs and desires to the restaurant staff to help make all of this happen.

The Restaurant Staff

- Maître d' (may-truh-DEE)—Oversees all the details that make things run smoothly in a restaurant. He takes reservations; greets customers; juggles seating arrangements; acts as a liaison between the kitchen and wait staff, and makes sure that everything looks as it should in the restaurant. He is also the one responsible for cultivating relationships with customers and making sure that they are happy.

- Captain/Headwaiter or waitress—Tells you the specials of the day, answers any questions you may have about items on the menu, and then takes your order.

- Sommelier (saw-muh-LYAH), or wine steward—Is the wine expert who puts together the wine list for a restaurant, maintains the wine cellar, and assists diners in the selection of wines to pair with their meals.

- Server—Is the person who brings the food to the table from the kitchen, places bread on the table, and refills the water glasses when necessary.

- Bartender: Responsible for tending the bar and mixing and pouring drinks for the wait staff to serve.

Did you know?

The first "doggie bags" were used around the 6th Century in ancient Rome. Dinner guests used their napkins to package foodstuffs to take home.

THE FINER POINTS:

* Know and use the "silent service code" for your dining utensils so that the wait staff will know if you are "resting" or are "finished" with a course.

* Be sure to let the wait staff know who host and guest of honor are if this applies.

* Ask the wait staff for an additional plate if you would like to share your food with a dining companion. (Never, however, ask a new client if they would like to share.)

* Make eye contact with the wait staff to let them know you need them at your table. If that doesn't work, make eye contact and put your index finger up to get their attention. Never call out to them across the room.

* Do say "please" and "thank-you" occasionally to the wait staff.

* Do ask for a takeaway bag, or "doggie bag" to take home leftover food if you are dining with your family or friends. Do not ask for one if you are dining with a client.

Did you know?

Emily Post did not approve of the practice of "doggie bags." In a newspaper column in 1968, she wrote: "I do not approve of taking leftover food such as pieces of meat from restaurants. Restaurants provide "doggie bags" for boxes to be taken to pets, and generally, the bags should be restricted to that use."

14

Gratuity Guidelines

"I like waiters to be attentive and smiling, as if they were having good friends over to their own house."
-Joel Robuchon, Restauranteur

Although tipping is considered voluntary in the United States, and the amount of the gratuity is up to the individual, it is expected and greatly appreciated by the restaurant staff who are often paid less than minimum wage. In some countries, a preset percentage may be added as a service charge, such as France, where a 15 percent service charge is automatically added to your bill by law. And, in the United States, restaurants often add a standard 20% service charge for large parties.

There are some countries, however, such as China, where a tip is not expected; and in Japan, there is no tipping, so it is considered rude to leave a tip. Whenever you are traveling to another country for business or pleasure, be sure to check the tipping guidelines before going.

Without a pleasant, well-trained and attentive restaurant staff, our dining experience at a restaurant would not be nearly as pleasurable, no matter how good the food or ambiance is. Most diners would, I believe, agree with Joel Robuchon, and would like for their waiters to be attentive and smiling. Showing them our respect and appreciation for a job well done, and for making our dining experience a pleasurable one—in the form of an appropriate gratuity—will keep them attentive and smiling.

Following are the standard tips currently for the restaurant staff when you are at an upscale restaurant in the United States:

- Maitre d' or Captain: $10.00 for special services, such as getting extra chairs and rearranging tables.

- Wait staff: 15 to 20% of the bill before tax.

- Bartender: 15 to 20%, or a minimum of $1 per drink.

- Sommelier: 10 to 15 % of the wine tab.

- Checkroom Attendant: $1.00 to $2.00 for each coat.

- Restroom Attendant: $1.00 if the attendant hands you a towel.

- Valet Parking Attendant: $2.00 per car.

Did you know?

Tipping was banned in six states—Washington, Mississippi, Arkansas, Tennessee, South Carolina, and Iowa—in the early 1900s. The punishment for the crime of soliciting or accepting a gratuity? A fine of $10 to $100, or up to thirty days of jail time.

Made in United States
Troutdale, OR
12/17/2023